W9-CUD-194

U.S.A. TRAVEL GUIDES

New Hampshire

BY ANN HEINRICHS · ILLUSTRATED BY MATT KANIA

Published by The Child's World®
1980 Lookout Drive • Mankato, MN 56003-1705
800-599-READ • www.childsworld.com

Photo Credits

Photographs ©: Olivier Le Queinec/Shutterstock Images, cover, 1; iStockphoto, 7, 31, 37 (bottom); Laura Stone/Shutterstock Images, 8; Peyman Zehtab Fard CC2.0, 11; Paul Tessier/Shutterstock Images, 12; Jim Cole/AP Images, 15; Lee Wright CC2.0, 16; Denis Tangney Jr./iStockphoto, 19; John Gollop/iStockphoto, 20; Shutterstock Images, 23, 37 (top); Jeffrey M. Frank/Shutterstock Images, 24; Craig Walsh/iStockphoto, 27; Cape Cod Photo/iStockphoto, 28; Jamie Gemmiti/The Conway Daily Sun/AP Images, 32; NASA Goddard Space Flight Center, 35

ISBN 9781503819696
LCCN 2016961182

Printing

Printed in the United States of America
PA02334

Ann Heinrichs is the author of more than 100 books for children and young adults. She has also enjoyed successful careers as a children's book editor and an advertising copywriter. Ann grew up in Fort Smith, Arkansas, and lives in Chicago, Illinois.

About the Author
Ann Heinrichs

Matt Kania loves maps and, as a kid, dreamed of making them. In school he studied geography and cartography, and today he makes maps for a living. Matt's favorite thing about drawing maps is learning about the places they represent. Many of the maps he has created can be found in books, magazines, videos, Web sites, and public places.

About the
Map Illustrator
Matt Kania

On the cover: Visit New Hampshire's state capitol in Concord.

OUR NEW HAMPSHIRE TRIP

NEW HAMPSHIRE

Let's tour New Hampshire! It's a great place to explore. Just look at all you'll do there.

You'll eat mooseburgers and seafood. You'll watch a star show. You'll see how waterwheels made factories run. You'll rattle up a mountain on a train. You'll meet bears, mountain lions, and moose. You'll pet bunnies and feed baby goats. And you'll watch people making maple syrup!

Just follow that loopy dotted line. Or make your own trip by skipping around. Either way, you're in for a big adventure. So buckle up and hang on tight. We're off to see New Hampshire!

WELCOME TO
NEW HAMPSHIRE

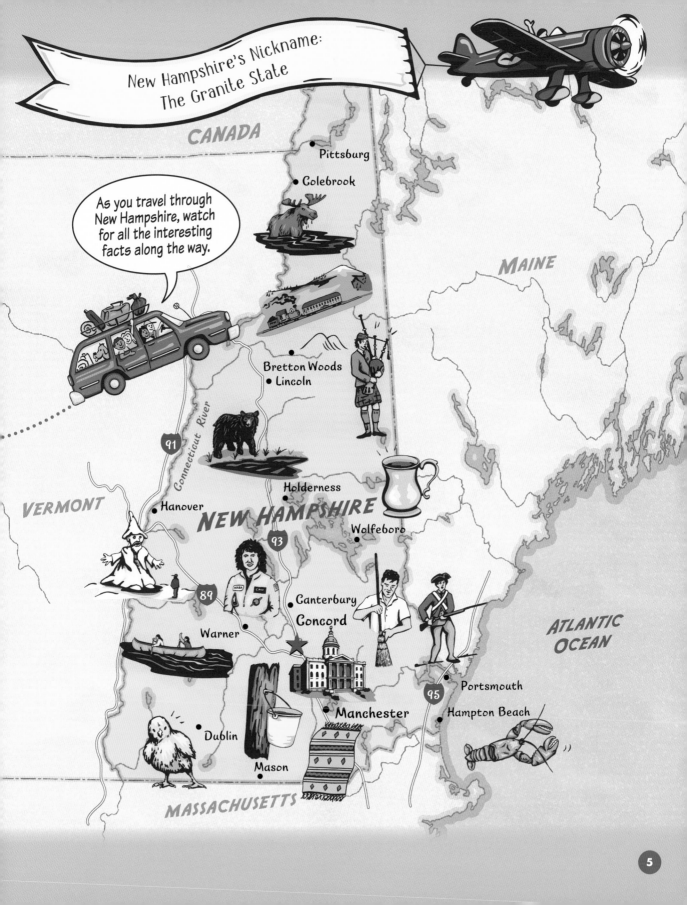

New Hampshire's Nickname:
The Granite State

CANADA

As you travel through New Hampshire, watch for all the interesting facts along the way.

Pittsburg

Colebrook

MAINE

Bretton Woods
Lincoln

Connecticut River

91

VERMONT

Hanover

NEW HAMPSHIRE

Holderness

Wolfeboro

93

89

Canterbury
Concord

Warner

ATLANTIC OCEAN

95

Portsmouth

Dublin

Manchester

Hampton Beach

Mason

MASSACHUSETTS

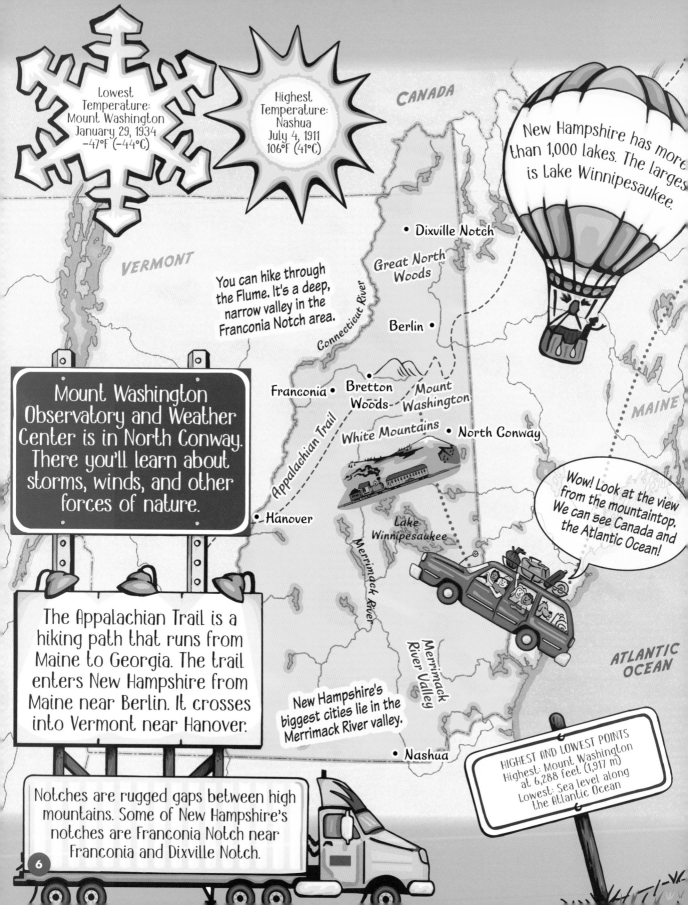

Lowest Temperature: Mount Washington January 29, 1934 -47°F (-44°C)

Highest Temperature: Nashua July 4, 1911 106°F (41°C)

CANADA

New Hampshire has more than 1,000 lakes. The largest is Lake Winnipesaukee.

• Dixville Notch

Great North Woods

VERMONT

You can hike through the Flume. It's a deep, narrow valley in the Franconia Notch area.

Connecticut River

Berlin •

Mount Washington Observatory and Weather Center is in North Conway. There you'll learn about storms, winds, and other forces of nature.

Franconia •   Bretton Woods   Mount Washington

Appalachian Trail

White Mountains   • North Conway

MAINE

Wow! Look at the view from the mountaintop. We can see Canada and the Atlantic Ocean!

• Hanover

Lake Winnipesaukee

The Appalachian Trail is a hiking path that runs from Maine to Georgia. The trail enters New Hampshire from Maine near Berlin. It crosses into Vermont near Hanover.

Merrimack River

Merrimack River Valley

ATLANTIC OCEAN

New Hampshire's biggest cities lie in the Merrimack River valley.

• Nashua

HIGHEST AND LOWEST POINTS
Highest: Mount Washington at 6,288 feet (1,917 m)
Lowest: Sea level along the Atlantic Ocean

Notches are rugged gaps between high mountains. Some of New Hampshire's notches are Franconia Notch near Franconia and Dixville Notch.

6

LOOKING OUT FROM MOUNT WASHINGTON

Take the little train up Mount Washington. You can get on in Bretton Woods. Mount Washington's slope is really steep! This is New Hampshire's highest peak. It's part of the rugged White Mountains. They cover north-central New Hampshire.

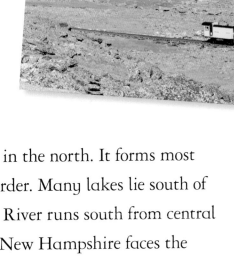

Look north from the mountaintop. You'll see the Great North Woods. Even farther north is Canada!

The Connecticut River rises in the north. It forms most of New Hampshire's western border. Many lakes lie south of the mountains. The Merrimack River runs south from central New Hampshire. Southeastern New Hampshire faces the Atlantic Ocean.

You can take a train to the top of Mount Washington. Be sure to take in the views!

THE HAMPTON BEACH SEAFOOD FESTIVAL

Chomp on some crunchy grilled shrimp. Scarf down a plate of fried clams. And how would you like your lobster? Broiled, fried, or served in a stew? You're at the Hampton Beach Seafood Festival!

New Hampshire has a short seacoast. It's only 18 miles (29 km) long. But people make the most of it. They enjoy beaches at Rye, New Castle, and Seabrook. Hampton Beach is the most popular spot. It's the perfect place for a seafood festival!

Try fried clams at the Hampton Beach Seafood Festival!

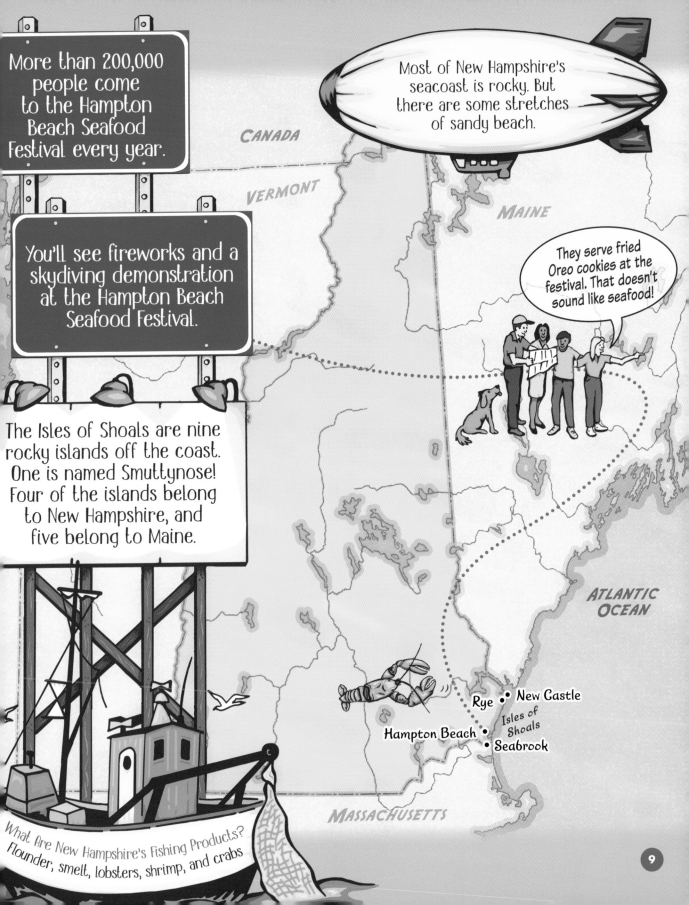

More than 200,000 people come to the Hampton Beach Seafood Festival every year.

You'll see fireworks and a skydiving demonstration at the Hampton Beach Seafood Festival.

The Isles of Shoals are nine rocky islands off the coast. One is named Smuttynose! Four of the islands belong to New Hampshire, and five belong to Maine.

Most of New Hampshire's seacoast is rocky. But there are some stretches of sandy beach.

They serve fried Oreo cookies at the festival. That doesn't sound like seafood!

CANADA

VERMONT

MAINE

ATLANTIC OCEAN

Rye • • New Castle
Isles of Shoals
Hampton Beach • •
• Seabrook

MASSACHUSETTS

What Are New Hampshire's Fishing Products?
Flounder, smelt, lobsters, shrimp, and crabs

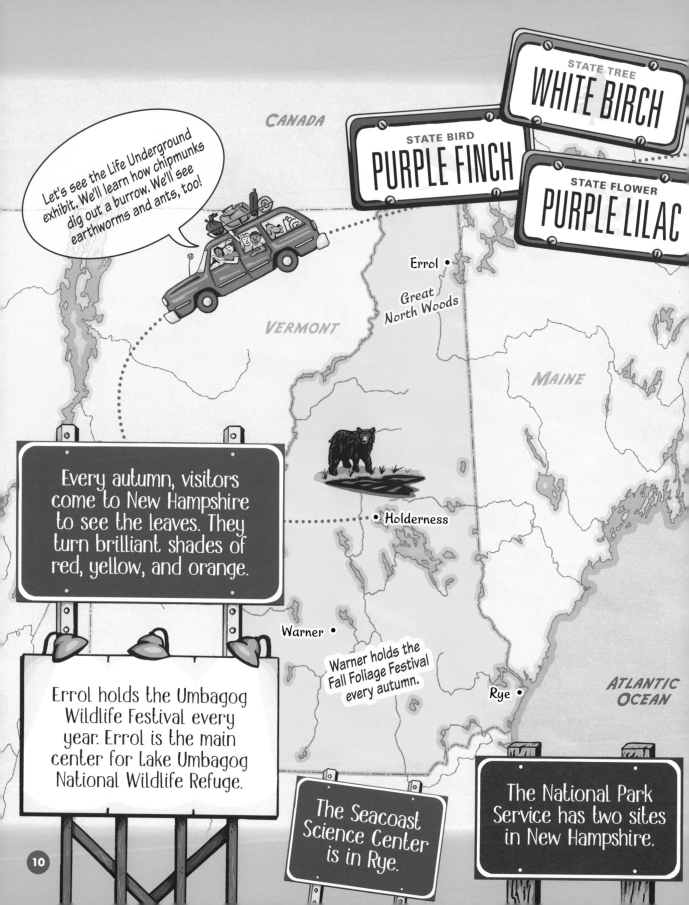

Let's see the Life Underground exhibit. We'll learn how chipmunks dig out a burrow. We'll see earthworms and ants, too!

STATE TREE
WHITE BIRCH

STATE BIRD
PURPLE FINCH

STATE FLOWER
PURPLE LILAC

CANADA

Errol •

Great
North Woods

VERMONT

MAINE

• Holderness

Every autumn, visitors come to New Hampshire to see the leaves. They turn brilliant shades of red, yellow, and orange.

Warner •

Warner holds the Fall Foliage Festival every autumn.

Rye •

ATLANTIC OCEAN

Errol holds the Umbagog Wildlife Festival every year. Errol is the main center for Lake Umbagog National Wildlife Refuge.

The Seacoast Science Center is in Rye.

The National Park Service has two sites in New Hampshire.

Meet the bears. Shh! One might be sleeping. Then check out the mountain lions. Eek! One might jump up right in front of you. You're exploring Squam Lakes Natural Science Center!

This nature center is in Holderness. Wander along its trails. You'll see otters, red foxes, and skunks. They're some of New Hampshire's many wild animals. Don't worry. Glass walls protect you from them.

Forests cover much of the state. Many animals make their homes there. They include deer, beavers, bobcats, and snowshoe hares. Moose live in the Great North Woods. So do black bears. It's fun to watch them from a safe distance!

This fox calls Squam Lakes Natural Science Center home.

THE NORTH COUNTRY MOOSE FESTIVAL

Want to try a juicy mooseburger? How about some delicious moose stew? You could try the moose-calling contest. Or just take a moose-watching tour. Where can you enjoy all these moose activities? At the North Country Moose Festival!

Big, shaggy moose live in the northern woods. So three towns decided to celebrate them. Colebrook and Pittsburg are two of the towns. The third town is nearby Canaan, Vermont. Together, they hold the moose festival every year!

Want to see lots of moose? Then travel along Moose Alley. It runs north from Pittsburg. Happy moose-watching!

There are nearly 4,000 moose in New Hampshire. Celebrate them at the North Country Moose Festival.

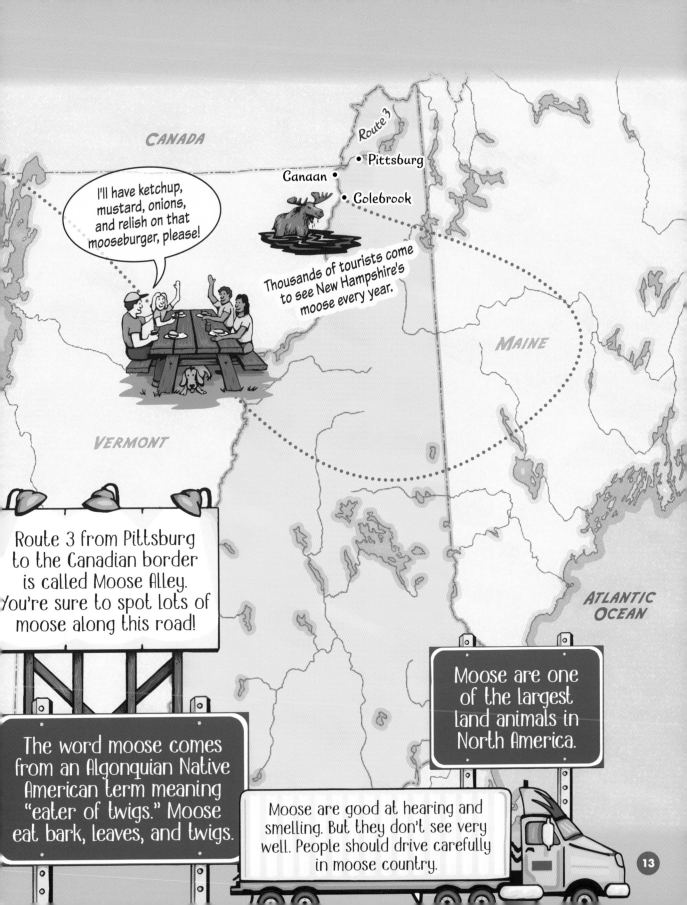

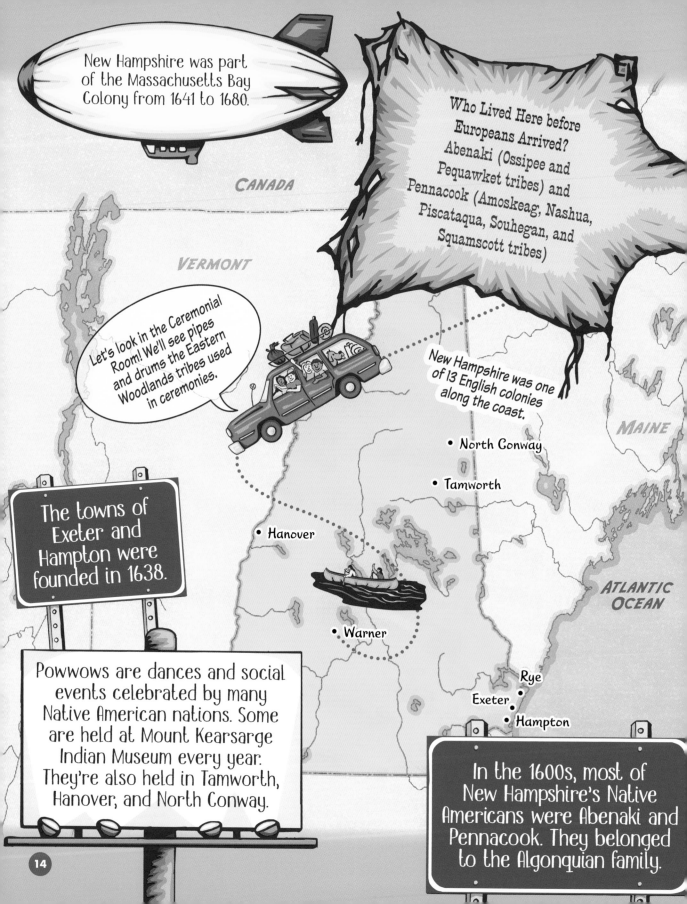

New Hampshire was part of the Massachusetts Bay Colony from 1641 to 1680.

Who Lived Here before Europeans Arrived? Abenaki (Ossipee and Pequawket tribes) and Pennacook (Amoskeag, Nashua, Piscataqua, Souhegan, and Squamscott tribes)

CANADA

VERMONT

Let's look in the Ceremonial Room! We'll see pipes and drums the Eastern Woodlands tribes used in ceremonies.

New Hampshire was one of 13 English colonies along the coast.

MAINE

• North Conway

• Tamworth

The towns of Exeter and Hampton were founded in 1638.

• Hanover

ATLANTIC OCEAN

• Warner

Rye

Exeter

• Hampton

Powwows are dances and social events celebrated by many Native American nations. Some are held at Mount Kearsarge Indian Museum every year. They're also held in Tamworth, Hanover, and North Conway.

In the 1600s, most of New Hampshire's Native Americans were Abenaki and Pennacook. They belonged to the Algonquian family.

MOUNT KEARSARGE INDIAN MUSEUM IN WARNER

Wander through Mount Kearsarge Indian Museum in Warner. You'll learn all about various Native American **cultures**. You'll see canoes, pottery, and religious objects.

Then follow the path through the Medicine Woods. Signs tell how the Mashpee Wampanoag Tribe used various plants. They used them for medicines, foods, and dyes.

Many Native Americans groups are from New Hampshire. They occupied the land for thousands of years before Europeans arrived. Many built homes with bark and animal skins. They hunted, fished, and farmed.

Englishman David Thomson arrived in 1623. He settled at Odiorne Point in what is now Rye. That was New Hampshire's first European settlement. New Hampshire became an English **colony**.

Want to learn about Native American cultures? Visit Mount Kearsarge Indian Museum!

STRAWBERY BANKE IN PORTSMOUTH

Stroll down the sunny lanes. Craftspeople are busy with their trades. You can try out some crafts yourself or play kids' games from the 1600s. You're visiting Strawbery Banke!

English colonists settled at Strawbery Banke in 1630. It grew into the busy seaport city of Portsmouth.

In time, the colonists became restless. Great Britain charged high taxes and controlled trade. New Hampshire decided to form its own government. It drew up its own **constitution**.

Colonists fought for freedom in the Revolutionary War (1775–1783). And they won! The colonies became the United States of America.

What was life like in the 1600s? Tour Strawbery Banke and find out!

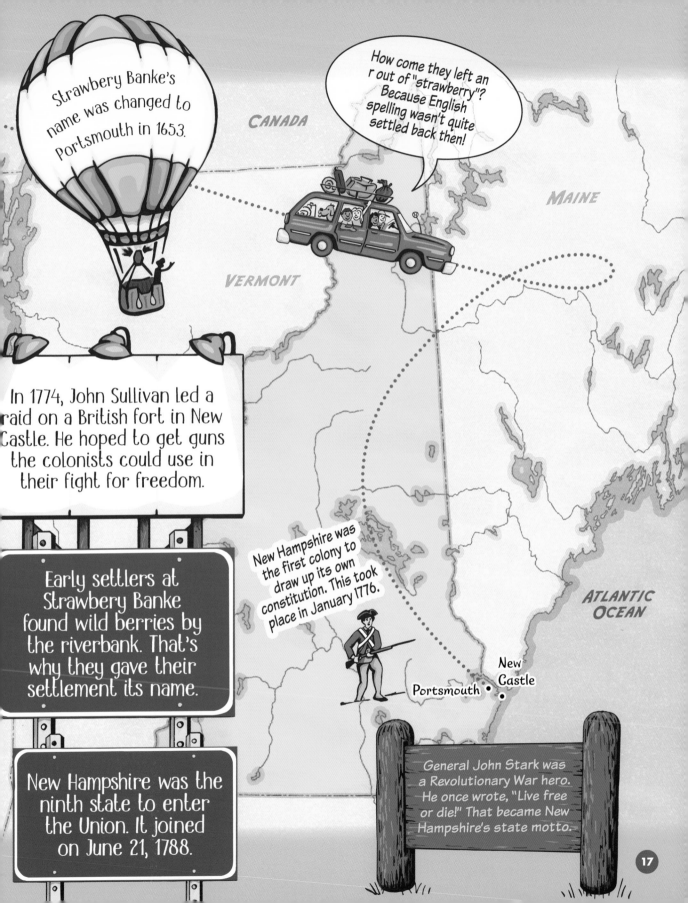

Strawbery Banke's name was changed to Portsmouth in 1653.

How come they left an r out of "strawberry"? Because English spelling wasn't quite settled back then!

CANADA

MAINE

VERMONT

In 1774, John Sullivan led a raid on a British fort in New Castle. He hoped to get guns the colonists could use in their fight for freedom.

Early settlers at Strawbery Banke found wild berries by the riverbank. That's why they gave their settlement its name.

New Hampshire was the first colony to draw up its own constitution. This took place in January 1776.

ATLANTIC OCEAN

New Hampshire was the ninth state to enter the Union. It joined on June 21, 1788.

New Castle

Portsmouth •

General John Stark was a Revolutionary War hero. He once wrote, "Live free or die!" That became New Hampshire's state motto.

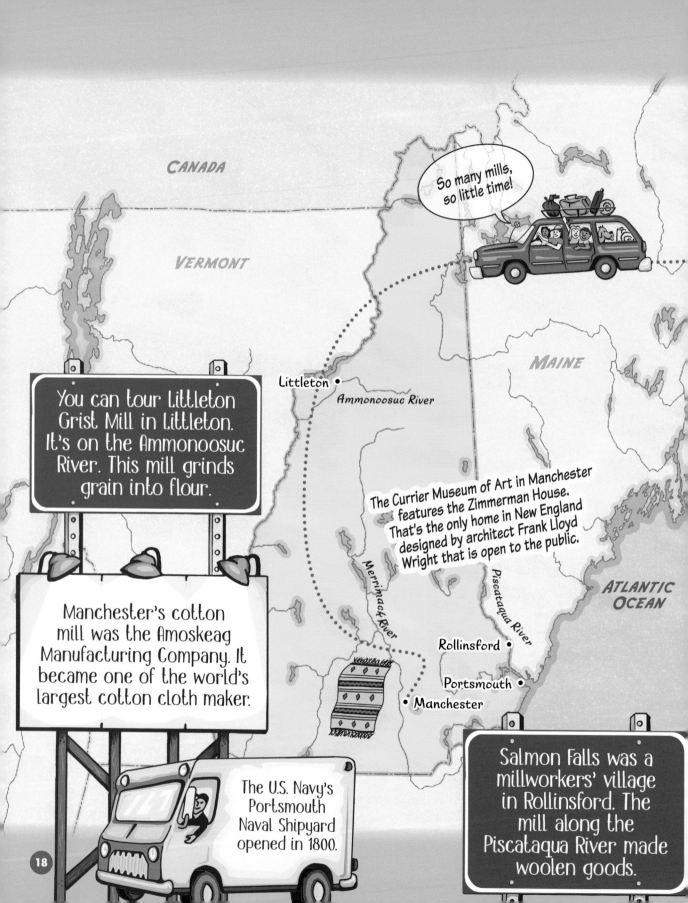

CANADA

VERMONT

MAINE

So many mills,
so little time!

Littleton •
Ammonoosuc River

You can tour Littleton Grist Mill in Littleton. It's on the Ammonoosuc River. This mill grinds grain into flour.

The Currier Museum of Art in Manchester features the Zimmerman House. That's the only home in New England designed by architect Frank Lloyd Wright that is open to the public.

ATLANTIC OCEAN

Merrimack River

Piscataqua River

Rollinsford •

Portsmouth •

• Manchester

Manchester's cotton mill was the Amoskeag Manufacturing Company. It became one of the world's largest cotton cloth maker.

The U.S. Navy's Portsmouth Naval Shipyard opened in 1800.

Salmon Falls was a millworkers' village in Rollinsford. The mill along the Piscataqua River made woolen goods.

MANCHESTER'S MILLYARD MUSEUM

Explore the Millyard Museum in Manchester. You'll learn how New Hampshire's early factories worked. This site was once a cotton mill. It stood beside the Merrimack River. The river's water turned a huge waterwheel. The wheel ran the mill's machines. They turned cotton into cloth.

New Hampshire's **industries** grew in the 1850s. Many mills and factories were built. Some made cotton or wool cloth. Others made boots and shoes. Sawmills made lumber and other wood products. Portsmouth became an important shipbuilding center, too.

Manchester became the state's biggest manufacturing center. Many **immigrants** came to work in the mills. Even children worked long hours there.

Learn about the history of New Hampshire's industries at the Millyard Museum.

HAMPSHIRE PEWTER IN WOLFEBORO

Most factories use machines to make things. But Hampshire Pewter in Wolfeboro makes things the old-fashioned way. Skilled craftspeople are hard at work there. And you can watch them!

First, workers mix tin with other metals. This produces pewter. Then they pour the melted metal into molds. Molds might be shaped like mugs, cups, or spoons. The gray metal hardens as it cools. Finally, the workers polish each piece.

New Hampshire had some of the nation's earliest factories. The state has grown with the times, though. Computer products are its major factory goods now!

Pewter is mostly made out of tin, as well as a little bit of copper.

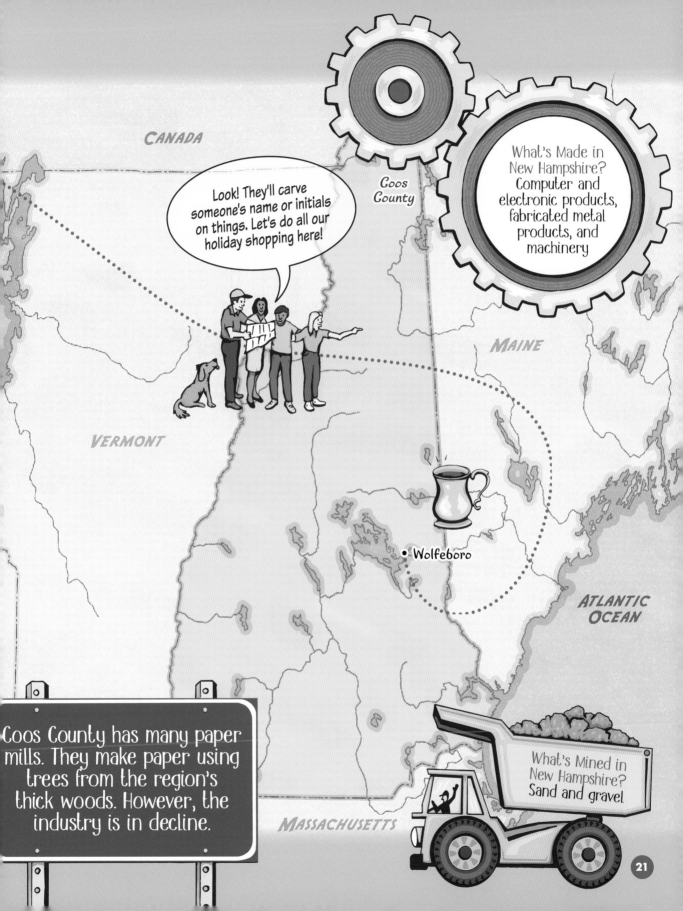

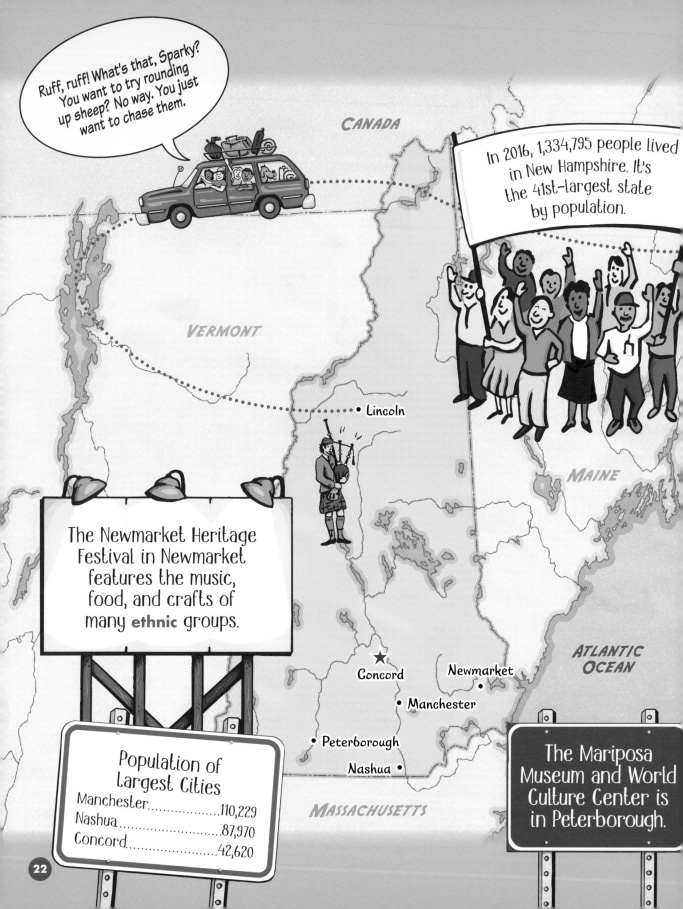

Ruff, ruff! What's that, Sparky? You want to try rounding up sheep? No way. You just want to chase them.

CANADA

In 2016, 1,334,795 people lived in New Hampshire. It's the 41st-largest state by population.

VERMONT

MAINE

• Lincoln

The Newmarket Heritage Festival in Newmarket features the music, food, and crafts of many **ethnic** groups.

ATLANTIC OCEAN

★ Concord

Newmarket •

• Manchester

Population of Largest Cities
Manchester.................110,229
Nashua.....................87,970
Concord....................42,620

• Peterborough

Nashua •

MASSACHUSETTS

The Mariposa Museum and World Culture Center is in Peterborough.

LINCOLN'S HIGHLAND GAMES AND FESTIVAL

Scottish step dancers prance across a stage. Harpists and bagpipers play **traditional** tunes. People push smooth stones across the ice. They're competing in an ancient game called curling. Sheepdogs compete in a contest, too. They show how well they round up sheep!

You're enjoying The New Hampshire Highland Games and Festival in Lincoln. It celebrates Scottish culture. New Hampshire welcomed many Scottish immigrants. Other immigrants came from Ireland, England, Wales, Germany, and Italy. French Canadians arrived from Canada, too. Many immigrants worked in the mills. Others opened shops or worked on farms.

The New Hampshire Highland Games and Festival is held the third weekend of September each year.

CANTERBURY SHAKER VILLAGE

New Hampshire's factories were buzzing with activity in the 1800s. But farms were thriving, too. Want a glimpse of farm life back then? Just visit Canterbury Shaker Village!

The Shakers were a religious group. They lived a simple farming life. All land and buildings belonged to the whole community. Everyone worked hard for the good of all.

You'll see many Shaker activities in the village. Some people are making brooms and boxes. Spinners and weavers are making clothes. You'll see the bee house and horse barn. In the bakery, check out the wood-burning oven. It baked 60 loaves of bread at once!

Be sure to visit the Syrup Shop. Different kinds of syrups and canned foods were made there!

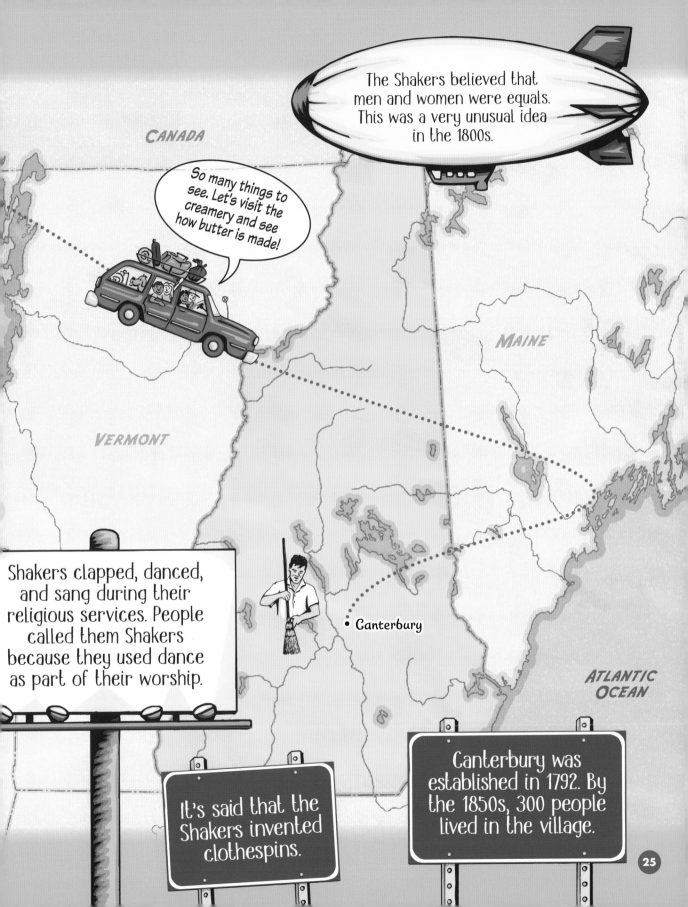

The Shakers believed that men and women were equals. This was a very unusual idea in the 1800s.

CANADA

So many things to see. Let's visit the creamery and see how butter is made!

MAINE

VERMONT

Shakers clapped, danced, and sang during their religious services. People called them Shakers because they used dance as part of their worship.

• Canterbury

ATLANTIC OCEAN

It's said that the Shakers invented clothespins.

Canterbury was established in 1792. By the 1850s, 300 people lived in the village.

There are several fairs in New Hampshire, including the Sandwich Fair held in Center Sandwich in October every year.

You can tour Stonyfield Farm Yogurt Works in Londonderry. It takes organic milk from dairy farmers and makes it into yogurt.

What Does New Hampshire Raise? Nursery and greenhouse products, dairy cattle, and beef cattle

I want to pet the bunnies! I want to hold the big, fat hen!

CANADA

VERMONT

MAINE

• Center Sandwich

The Hopkinton State Fair is held in Contoocook in September each year.

• Milton

Milton is home to the New Hampshire Farm Museum.

• Contoocook

• Deerfield

• Dublin

• Londonderry

ATLANTIC OCEAN

Deerfield holds the Sheep and Wool Festival every year.

Hold a fluffy chick. Feed a baby goat. Oink with the pigs. Or cuddle a fleecy lamb. You're visiting the Friendly Farm in Dublin!

You'll get friendly with the farm animals here. The farmers are friendly, too. They hope you'll love farming as they do!

Many New Hampshire farmers raise dairy cows. Their milk is made into butter and ice cream. Hay is the major field crop. It's used as animal feed. Apples are important crops, too. The top farm products are not foods, though. They're plants for people's homes. That includes Christmas trees!

Oink, oink! Check out the pigs at the Friendly Farm!

PARKER'S MAPLE BARN IN MASON

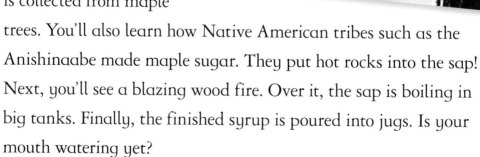

Is it early spring? Do you smell something sweet in the air? You must be near a sugarhouse! That's where people make maple syrup.

Many New Hampshire sugarhouses give tours. One is Parker's Maple Barn in Mason. There you'll learn all about making maple syrup. You'll see how **sap** is collected from maple trees. You'll also learn how Native American tribes such as the Anishinaabe made maple sugar. They put hot rocks into the sap! Next, you'll see a blazing wood fire. Over it, the sap is boiling in big tanks. Finally, the finished syrup is poured into jugs. Is your mouth watering yet?

Yum, maple syrup! See how it's made at Parker's Maple Barn.

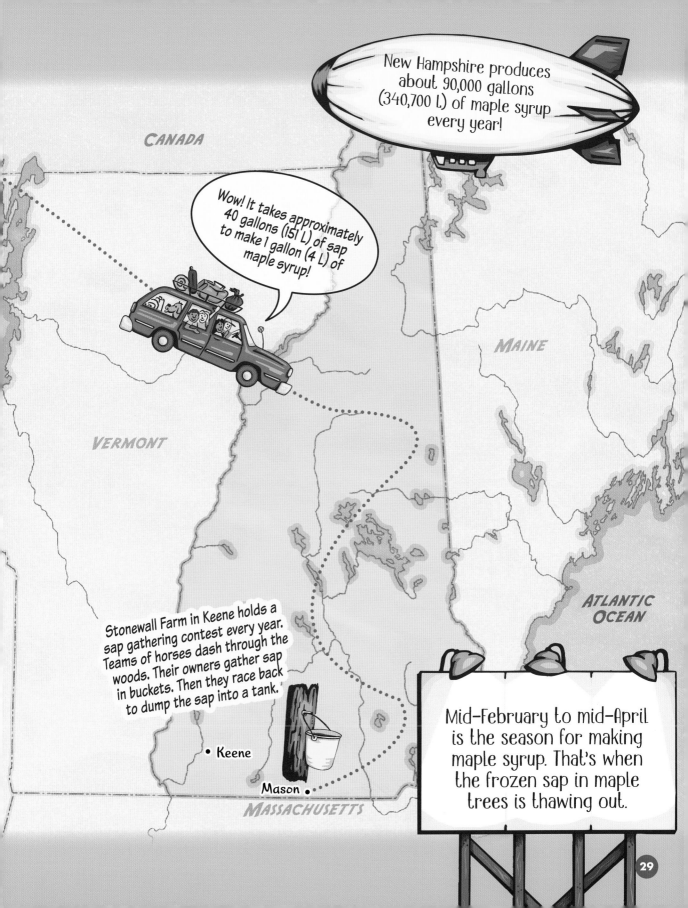

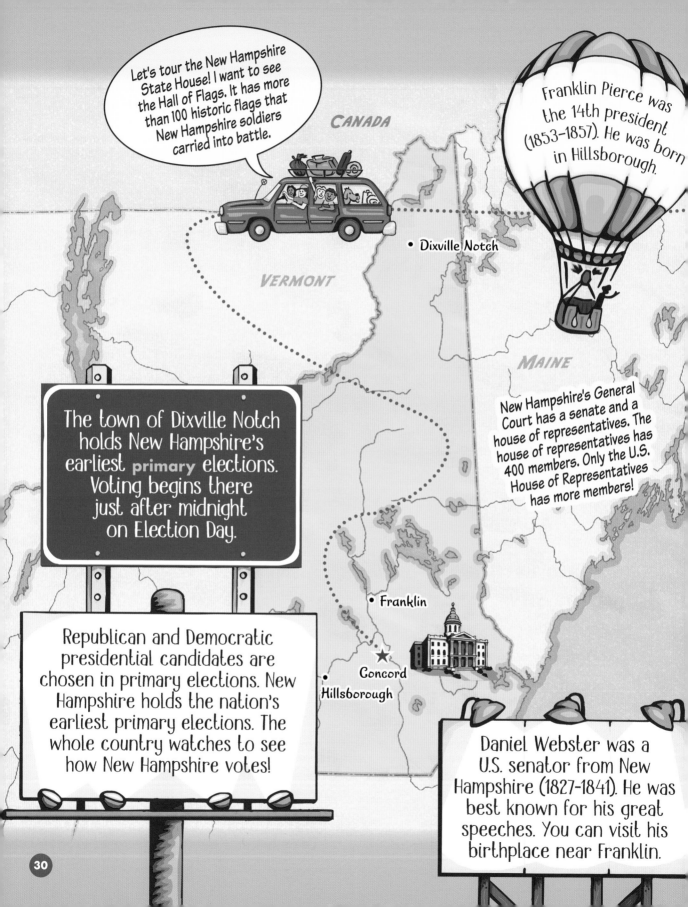

Let's tour the New Hampshire State House! I want to see the Hall of Flags. It has more than 100 historic flags that New Hampshire soldiers carried into battle.

Franklin Pierce was the 14th president (1853–1857). He was born in Hillsborough.

CANADA

VERMONT

• Dixville Notch

MAINE

New Hampshire's General Court has a senate and a house of representatives. The house of representatives has 400 members. Only the U.S. House of Representatives has more members!

The town of Dixville Notch holds New Hampshire's earliest **primary** elections. Voting begins there just after midnight on Election Day.

• Franklin

★ Concord

• Hillsborough

Republican and Democratic presidential candidates are chosen in primary elections. New Hampshire holds the nation's earliest primary elections. The whole country watches to see how New Hampshire votes!

Daniel Webster was a U.S. senator from New Hampshire (1827–1841). He was best known for his great speeches. You can visit his birthplace near Franklin.

THE STATE CAPITOL IN CONCORD

What's the capitol made of? Granite, of course! New Hampshire is called the Granite State. It has huge deposits of this building stone. Granite is strong and solid. It's beautiful, too!

It's a good thing the capitol, also known as the New Hampshire State House, is solid. It houses the state government offices. New Hampshire's government has three branches. One branch makes the state's laws. It's called the General Court. Another branch makes sure laws are obeyed. This branch is headed by the governor. Judges make up the third branch. They decide whether someone has broken the law.

The New Hampshire State House is the oldest capitol in which the legislature still meets in the original chamber.

THE DARTMOUTH WINTER CARNIVAL IN HANOVER

Gaze at the ice sculptures. Most are bigger than you! Then check out the polar bear swim. You won't spot any polar bears, though. You'll see people who aren't wearing very much. They jump into icy water for a swim!

This is the Dartmouth Winter Carnival in Hanover. It's one of New Hampshire's many winter festivals. Winter also brings in thousands of skiers. They ski the snowy slopes of the White Mountains.

There's plenty to do when it's warmer, too. Some people enjoy the seaside beaches. And some just drive around. They admire the little villages and the colorful leaves.

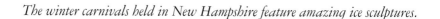

The winter carnivals held in New Hampshire feature amazing ice sculptures.

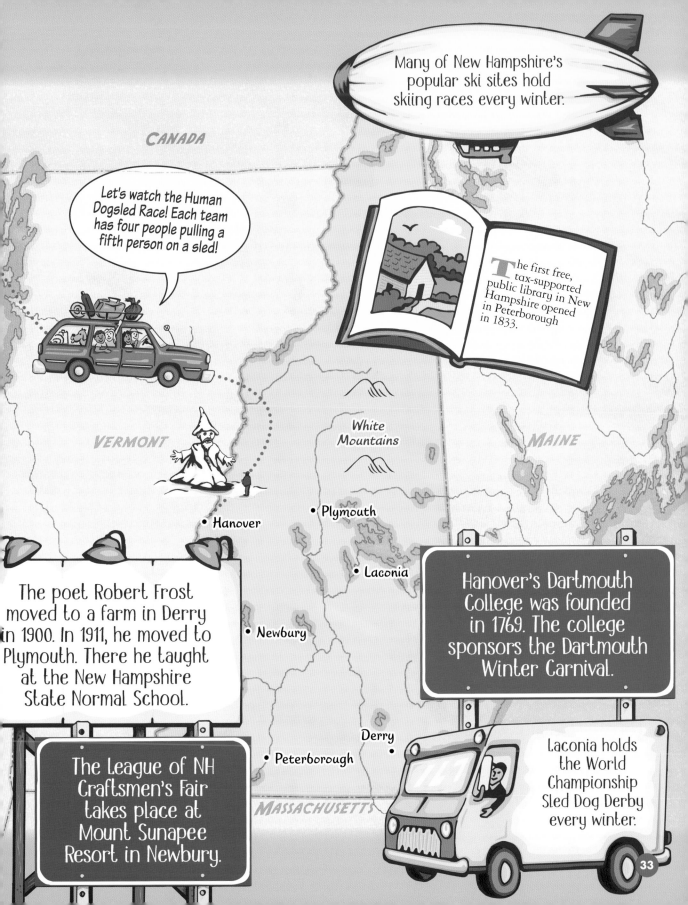

Many of New Hampshire's popular ski sites hold skiing races every winter.

Let's watch the Human Dogsled Race! Each team has four people pulling a fifth person on a sled!

The first free, tax-supported public library in New Hampshire opened in Peterborough in 1833.

CANADA

VERMONT

MAINE

White Mountains

• Plymouth

• Hanover

• Laconia

The poet Robert Frost moved to a farm in Derry in 1900. In 1911, he moved to Plymouth. There he taught at the New Hampshire State Normal School.

Hanover's Dartmouth College was founded in 1769. The college sponsors the Dartmouth Winter Carnival.

• Newbury

Derry

• Peterborough

MASSACHUSETTS

The League of NH Craftsmen's Fair takes place at Mount Sunapee Resort in Newbury.

Laconia holds the World Championship Sled Dog Derby every winter.

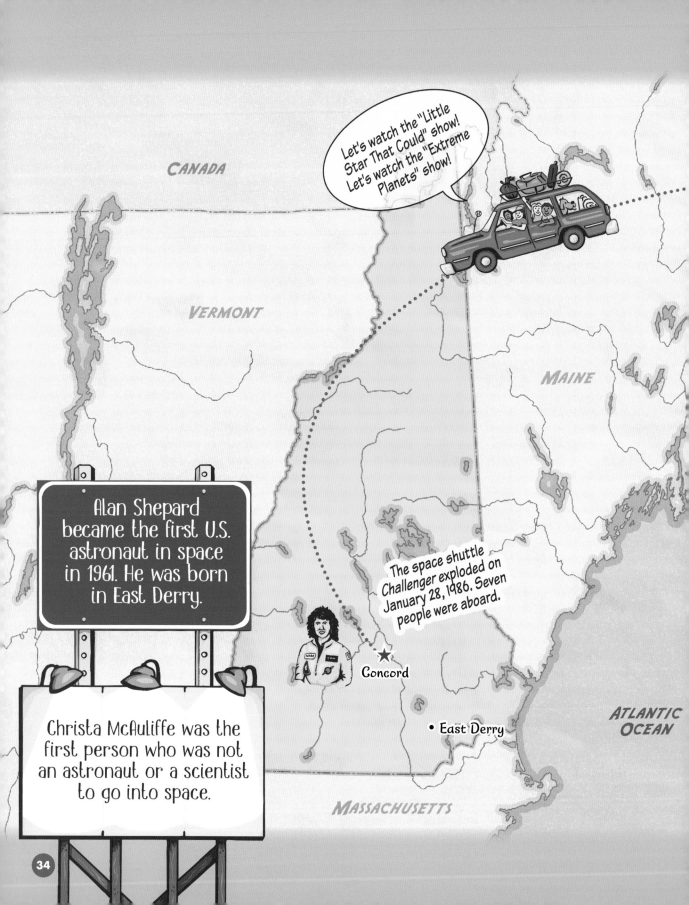

Let's watch the "Little Star That Could" show! Let's watch the "Extreme Planets" show!

CANADA

VERMONT

MAINE

Alan Shepard became the first U.S. astronaut in space in 1961. He was born in East Derry.

The space shuttle Challenger exploded on January 28, 1986. Seven people were aboard.

Concord

East Derry

ATLANTIC OCEAN

Christa McAuliffe was the first person who was not an astronaut or a scientist to go into space.

MASSACHUSETTS

CONCORD'S McAULIFFE-SHEPARD DISCOVERY CENTER

Lean back and watch the night sky unfold. Which objects are stars? Which are planets? What patterns do the stars make? You'll learn all this and more. You're at the McAuliffe-Shepard Discovery Center's planetarium. And you're watching an exciting sky show!

Who was Christa McAuliffe? She was a schoolteacher in Concord. She was chosen to fly aboard the space shuttle *Challenger*. The whole country was excited. But the shuttle exploded after takeoff. Everyone aboard was killed.

Christa McAuliffe loved teaching kids. This center was built in her honor. It's a great place to carry on her work!

Christa McAuliffe, top row second from the left, and the crew of the Challenger

OUR TRIP

We visited many amazing places on our trip! We also met a lot of interesting people along the way. Look at the map below. Use your finger to trace all the places we have been.

What is the largest lake in New Hampshire? *Page 6 has the answer.*

How many islands make up the Isles of Shoals? *See page 9 for the answer.*

Where is Moose Alley? *Look on page 13 for the answer.*

What are powwows? *Page 14 has the answer.*

How did Strawbery Banke get its name? *Turn to page 17 for the answer.*

What kind of mills can you find in Coos County? *Look on page 21 for the answer.*

What is said to have been invented by the Shakers? *Page 25 has the answer.*

What town holds the World Championship Sled Dog Derby? *Turn to page 33 for the answer.*

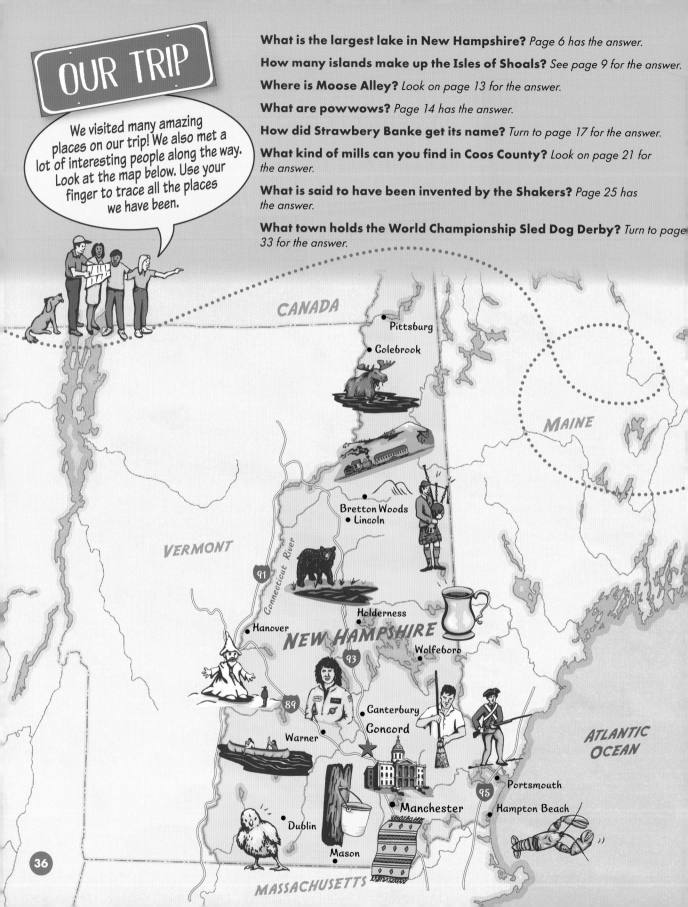

CANADA

Pittsburg

Colebrook

MAINE

VERMONT

Bretton Woods
Lincoln

Connecticut River

91

Holderness

Hanover

NEW HAMPSHIRE

Wolfeboro

93

89

Canterbury

Concord

Warner

ATLANTIC OCEAN

95

Portsmouth

Hampton Beach

Manchester

Dublin

Mason

MASSACHUSETTS

STATE SYMBOLS

State amphibian: Red-spotted newt

State animal: White-tailed deer

State bird: Purple finch

State butterfly: Karner blue

State flower: Purple lilac

State freshwater fish: Brook trout

State insect: Ladybug

State mineral: Beryl

State rock: Granite

State saltwater fish: Striped bass

State sport: Skiing

State tree: White birch

State wildflower: Pink lady's slipper

STATE SONG

"OLD NEW HAMPSHIRE"

Words by Dr. John F. Holmes, music by Maurice Hoffmann

With a skill that knows no measure,
From the golden store of Fate
God, in His great love and wisdom,
Made the rugged Granite State;
Made the lakes, the fields, the forests;
Made the Rivers and the rills;
Made the bubbling, crystal fountains
Of New Hampshire's Granite Hills.

Chorus:
Old New Hampshire, Old New Hampshire

Old New Hampshire Grand and Great
We will sing of Old New Hampshire,
Of the dear old Granite State.

Builded he New Hampshire glorious
From the borders to the sea;
And with matchless charm and splendor
Blessed her for eternity.
Hers, the majesty of mountain;
Hers, the grandeur of the lake;
Hers, the truth as from the hillside
Whence her crystal waters break.
(Chorus)

State seal

That was a great trip! We have traveled all over New Hampshire! There are a few places that we didn't have time for, though. Next time, we plan to visit the Children's Museum of New Hampshire. Visitors enjoy a variety of activities, including digging for fossils and playing African drums. If we have time, we can even take a trolley ride!

State flag

FAMOUS PEOPLE

Beach, Amy Marcy Cheney (1867–1944), pianist and composer

Brown, Alice (1856–1948), author

Burns, Ken (1953–), documentary filmmaker

Chase, Salmon P. (1808–1873), politician and jurist

Cochran, Barbara (1951–), Olympic skier

Eddy, Mary Baker (1821–1910), founder of the Christian Science Church

Fisk, Carlton (1947–), former baseball player

Flynn, Elizabeth Gurley (1890–1964), founding member of the American Civil Liberties Union

Frost, Robert (1874–1963), poet

Greeley, Horace (1811–1872), journalist and political leader

Irving, John (1942–), author

Jacobi, Lotte (1896–1990), photographer

McAuliffe, Christa (1948–1986), teacher and astronaut

Montana, Bob (1920–1975), Archie comics cartoonist

Pierce, Franklin (1804–1869), 14th U.S. president

Porter, Eleanor (1868–1920), children's author

Salinger, J. D. (1919–2010), author

Sandler, Adam (1966–), actor and comedian

Shepard, Alan, Jr. (1923–1998), astronaut

Tupper, Earl (1907–1983), inventor of Tupperware

Webster, Daniel (1782–1852), lawyer and statesman

WORDS TO KNOW

colony (KOL-uh-nee) a land with ties to a parent country

constitution (kon-stuh-TOO-shuhn) a statement of the basic laws and ideas that govern a state or nation

cultures (KUHL-churs) the beliefs, customs, and ways of life of different groups of people

ethnic (ETH-nik) relating to a person's race or nationality

immigrants (IM-uh-gruhnts) people who move to another country

industries (IN-duh-streez) types of businesses

primary (PRYE-mair-ee) first or earliest

sap (SAP) the liquid that circulates within a plant

traditional (truh-DISH-uh-nuhl) following long-held customs

TO LEARN MORE

IN THE LIBRARY

Marsh, Carole. *I'm Reading about New Hampshire.* Peachtree City, GA: Gallopade International, 2011.

Rissman, Rebecca. *What's Great about New Hampshire?* Minneapolis, MN: Lerner Publications, 2015.

Rowland, Wickie. *Good Morning, Strawbery Banke.* Portsmouth, NH: Peter E. Randall Publisher, 2010.

ON THE WEB

Visit our Web site for links about New Hampshire:

childsworld.com/links

Note to Parents, Teachers, and Librarians: We routinely verify our Web links to make sure they are safe and active sites. So encourage your readers to check them out!

PLACES TO VISIT OR CONTACT

New Hampshire Division of Travel and Tourism Development

visitnh.gov

172 Pembroke Road

Concord, NH 03301

603/271-2665

For more information about traveling in New Hampshire

New Hampshire Historical Society

nhhistory.org

30 Park Street

Concord, NH 03301

603/228-6688

For more information about the history of New Hampshire

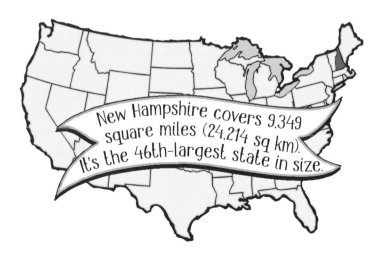

New Hampshire covers 9,349 square miles (24,214 sq km). It's the 46th-largest state in size.

INDEX

Bye, Granite State.
We had a great time.
We'll be back soon!